W9-COD-835

CENTRAL ELEMENTARY SCHOOL

DODD, MEAD WONDER BOOKS

Wonders
of the
Monkey World

MONKEYS AND APES IN THE WILD

Jacquelyn Berrill

ILLUSTRATED BY
THE AUTHOR

DODD, MEAD & COMPANY, NEW YORK

To all my family

IN APPRECIATION

This book could not have been written without the help of the scientists who have gone to the tropical rain forests to study monkeys and apes and who have then published scientific papers about their findings. The list is far too long to give here, but it includes scientists from all over the world — Europe, Asia and America. To all of them I wish to express my deep appreciation.

JACQUELYN BERRILL

Contents

I

Where Monkeys Live

TROPICAL RAIN FORESTS

Have you ever noticed that the largest crowd at the zoo is usually standing in front of a monkey cage? We all, young and old, enjoy watching these fascinating creatures. We laugh at them because they remind us of ourselves—a mother monkey reaches out to pull a thumb from her infant's sucking mouth; a baby climbs too high on the wires and a frightened cry brings the mother to its side. It is always hard to leave the monkey section of the zoo. No other animals, large or small, hold our interest so long or draw us back so often.

The monkeys you watch in the zoo are cramped and live unnatural lives. No matter how good the zoological garden is, a zoo home is a far cry from their real homes in the tops of trees in the rain forests. Of course it is only under these caged conditions that we are able to watch these fascinating creatures at all. However, this book is not about their zoo homes, but how the monkeys and apes live their lives in their native habitat, swinging through the branches of the tallest trees in the rain forests.

Today, many scientists go into these dense forests to study monkeys. They stay months, sometimes even years, following a monkey band or family about, day and night. They build blinds, or hiding shelters, in the treetops to get closer looks and to take photographs. Often the monkeys become so accustomed to see-

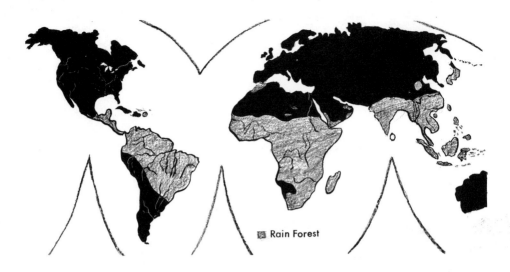

Rain Forest

ing their human visitors that they accept them as members of the family.

These scientists keep records and afterwards write scientific papers describing all they have learned about the wild, free lives of the monkeys. It is from these accounts that we are able to find out how the monkeys and apes really live in the forests around the world.

Monkeys live in tropical forests where the heavy rainfall all the year round makes the forest grow tall and dense. The 150-foot trees form a thick canopy overhead, like a tent, with some giants of 200 feet towering above. Little sun gets through the heavy foliage and as a result the vegetation on the ground has to struggle to grow and is less dense. Here we find a covering of ferns, dwarf palms, tree seedlings and thickets of broad-leaf plants that need little light and are related to the plants your mother grows in a dimly lit corner at home.

Monkeys are found in the tropical rain forests of South America, Africa and Asia. They live in their treetop world together with any other animals that are able to climb so high. Creatures that have claws to climb and cling with, or have feet or tails

8

that can grasp like hands, can manage to live here. Frogs have suction pads on their toes, while snails make use of a sticky slime on their journey upward. Of course, any animal that can jump, glide, or fly can reach the safety of the tall, dense canopy overhead.

When the monkeys come down to the leaf-and-fern-covered floor of the rain forest they meet other animals, large and small. Elephants, buffalo, leopards and dwarf antelopes—to name but a few—live under the African tree canopy. The tapir and jaguar roam the ground in the American tropical rain forests and wild hogs root about in the soil.

Tiny deer, no larger than rabbits, inhabit the Oriental forests of the Old World. Frogs and toads thrive in the moist air and brilliant butterflies and birds find the rain forests around the world ideal for their way of life. You can see that the monkey world is filled with activity, songs and color.

Some monkeys live as far north as Japan, while the "Barbary apes" are found at Gibraltar. But most monkeys and apes live in the tropics, where they can find insects, seeds, tubers, leaves, and fruit all the year long. Monkeys cannot migrate as birds do, nor can they hibernate or store food. They must be able to find food nearby every day of the year. Rain forests fill their needs, for there is plenty of water, shelter and food all the year around, and thus they are ideal for the monkey's way of life.

There are two principal kinds of monkeys—Old World and New World. The New World monkeys live in the Americas and usually have long, prehensile (grasping) tails that are used like an extra hand. The Old World monkeys live in Africa and Asia and *never* have tails that are prehensile, but generally have brightly colored buttocks. Both Old and New World monkeys are arboreal, which means they live in the treetops, except for the baboons who have taken to living in open country on the

9

ground, and macaques that spend much time on the ground within the forests.

A long time ago monkeys inhabited most of Europe, Central Russia and the Middle East, but this was before the glacial ice covered the land and swept away the great trees which gave them shelter and food. Today, no monkeys live in Europe except the so-called "Barbary apes" that were probably brought to Gibraltar by the Arabs when they conquered Spain. All Old World monkeys live in Africa and Asia south of the Himalaya mountains, except those that are found in Japan. Wherever there are tropical rain forests you will find monkeys swinging through the treetops, calling loudly or quietly chattering to each other.

2

Pre-Monkeys

Long before there were any real monkeys, as we know them, there were small, shy, gentle monkey-like creatures that lived in the treetops. By day they hid in the dense foliage and slept. When night came, the tiny animals, protected by darkness, ventured out to find food. They clung to branches with curved toenails or with toe pads, and were well adapted to their way of life. They had large eyes that gathered all the light available, and had large ears that could twist and turn for hearing the slightest sound. Once, very long ago, these small creatures of the night were common in the warm forests all over the world, but that was before the more aggressive monkeys, who are related to them, came into existence and began to hunt them, forcing them into isolated places of safety. These "pre-monkeys," as they are called, are now represented only by the spectral tarsier of Indonesia and the Philippine Islands, by the lemurs of the island of Madagascar, and by lemur-like creatures in Africa and Southeast Asia.

LEMUR

The mouse lemur, only four inches long, is the smallest of a group that varies in size, shape and habits. These tiny creatures build nests of twigs and leaves in the tall trees of the damp forests and spend most of the time leaping about hunting food.

Mouse lemur

Sifaka lemur

However, for a part of the year they are inactive and live on the stored-up fat under the skin at the base of the tail.

The lemur that is best known is the sifaka—often called the "monkey lemur." A family of monkeys wearing long fluffy coats with white cowls that frame their black faces travels together through the treetops eating fruits, flowers, leaves and bark. They keep together in the thick growth by making a sound much like a "hiccup."

The family sometimes comes down to the ground to play. Scientists have been able to watch these monkeys leaping about on their long, thin legs. But the lemurs know that safety lies in the treetops and when the alarmed call of *she-fak*—from which they get their name—is given, they disappear in the dense foliage overhead.

Aye-aye

AYE-AYE

Until recently, the aye-aye was thought to be extinct but then a scientist found one of them curled up in a nest of leaves. The

13

creature, about the size of a cat with a huge tail, lives its solitary life in dense forests and giant bamboo thickets. Besides fruit and bamboo, the aye-aye eats insects which it digs from bark with a long, thin middle finger.

Slow loris

SLOW LORIS

Slow loris is too shy to be seen easily. It comes out at night and slowly moves about feeding. Sometimes the creature hangs by its feet, thus freeing its hands for catching insects. "Loris" means clown so the slow loris, or slow clown, is well named.

Potto

POTTO

Natives of Africa call the potto "softly-softly" because it moves slowly and deliberately. But the potto can hurry when alarmed and nature gave the animal a very effective weapon in the form of pointed bones that stick through the skin at the back of the neck. When a potto becomes angry it flips its head down and butts with its neck.

15

Bush baby

BUSH BABY

There's nothing slow about bush babies as they leap wildly from branch to branch, using their bushy tails as balancers in their nightly acrobatics. These tiny, soft, furry animals have very large eyes and ears that can be turned about independently. On each tiny finger and toe there is a fleshy pad that helps them cling safely to limbs as they jump about hunting food.

TARSIER

The tarsier, another tiny (2½ or 3 inches), soft, furry night animal, has survived unchanged for sixty million years on some of the Southeast Asian islands, Sumatra, Java, Borneo, and the Philippines. It, too, owes its survival to its habit of hiding by day in holes at the tops of trees or in matted vines. When dark comes, the animal clings tightly with special toe pads to branches as it waits for the unsuspecting insect or lizard to come along. A tarsier can twist its head all the way around to see what is coming up behind.

Tarsier

3

True Monkeys

Monkeys are very well made for their particular way of life. Living in the treetops calls for exceptionally good vision, without which the first leap from limb to limb could result in a fatal fall. When you jump from one place to another, you judge the distance before you leap, and so must a monkey. Judging the distance to the nearest landing calls for binocular vision (the ability to see one object in front of another), which monkeys, apes and men all possess. Monkeys and apes live in a world of color and they share with man and the birds, and some other creatures, a wonderful sense of color vision. On the other hand, their sense of smell is not very good, but then, living in the treetops far above the ground, the sense of smell is unimportant. Only animals that live on the ground have special need of it.

Animals living high among the trees need to be able to cling tightly to the branches, for their very life depends on it. So monkeys and apes have grasping hands (and feet) with opposable thumbs—that is, with thumbs that can be held opposite the fingers so as to grasp a branch or some small object.

Have you ever really looked at your own very wonderful hand? See how your thumb and forefinger work together to pick up a pin. In catching a ball, your fingers spread out to form a sort of cup. Now hold your fingers stiff to pick up a paper or a spoon, or button your coat or comb your hair. You can see

18

how well your hands manipulate all kinds of things and that without such hands, and the marvelous eyes that guide them, you wouldn't be at all the same. And so it is with the monkey, although its hands are not so good as yours. Yet they are well made for clinging to branches and at the same time are able to reach out to pluck fruit to eat. Good-enough hands and distance-judging vision have enabled monkeys to survive among the forest treetops for many millions of years.

4

New World Monkeys

The New World monkeys live in the great rain forests of Central and South America where the trees are thick and tall and the foliage is dense. The monkeys in the New World are only distantly related to those in the Old World (Africa and Asia), for they are probably descended from different pre-monkey ancestors. Of course, they have much in common, but there is one big difference. Only New World monkeys can hang by their tails. They alone possess wonderful prehensile (grasping) tails which they use as an extra hand.

Much study has been made of the monkeys living in the Panama Canal Zone, especially those on Barro Colorado Island. Troops of monkeys were observed for hours every day by scientists carrying field glasses, compasses, cameras, notebooks and snake antitoxins. Camouflaged blinds were built of burlap and brush, in trees and on the ground, at places visited by the troop being studied. Anything strange causes the monkeys to act abnormally. They either flee or else the males come forward vocalizing aggressively. After many weeks, human investigators are usually accepted by the monkeys, who seem to realize that such scientists are not enemies with guns.

It would be fun if we could follow the scientist as he studies each kind of monkey, but then we would have to make a separate book for each animal. Let's get acquainted with certain characters in the monkey world and meet others in only a pic-

A howler monkey greets the dawn

ture and a sentence or two. All monkeys are interesting and the more you know about them the more fascinating they become.

HOWLER MONKEY

As the first faint glow of light appears in the eastern sky, a large, male reddish-brown howler monkey sits upright in the tallest tree and breaks the deep silence with a tremendous howl. Some distance away another howler responds. The ear-splitting noise carries far across the dense forest as the responding calls spread to numerous groups of howlers, sounding like the roll of distant thunder. Dawn has arrived in the rain forest and has been greeted as only howler monkeys can greet it.

We do not know whether the loud roars say to other creatures in the forest "stay away from my territory" or "I'm fierce, hear my roar." At any rate, each group of howlers does have a limited territory in which they roam freely from the lodge trees, where they sleep, to the feeding trees, heavy with leaves and fruit. Howlers prefer the tallest trees in the very densest part of the forest where they can instantly disappear in the heavy foliage if need arises. They are heavy, bulky animals that move majestically through the trees, although on occasion they can travel faster than can a scientist on the ground. Howler monkeys, however, are ill equipped for travel except in the tall trees. Scrub, made up of smaller trees and shrubs, cannot hold the howlers' weight and they are forced to live far above in the treetops.

After about thirty minutes of the early morning community howling, the male leader gives a series of deep hoarse clucks and moves off along a limb, followed by the rest of the troop in single file. Their progress is slow and deliberate and easy to follow. Their route is a well-traveled one and is the shortest way to their feeding trees. The animals walk along the upper side of limbs on all fours, with hands divided over a branch, two fingers on one side and three on the other. You see, howler monkeys do not have hands with an opposable thumb such as you and many monkeys have. Instead, they have opposable great toes which make their hind feet even more handlike than their forefeet, suitable for grasping branches and vines. Howlers also have prehensile tails which serves as a fifth hand, for use in anchoring themselves in the treetops during sleep and rest, and for grasping nearby branches to steady themselves as they move through the trees.

There were twenty-six howlers in one group studied by scientists. Three were males, seven were females without infants, eight were juveniles, and four were mothers carrying babies. One baby was so young it clung to the hair on its mother's chest, two rode piggyback, with their own tails coiled round the base of the mother's tail, and the other walked close to its mother along the branches. Sometimes progress from the end of one branch to the beginning of another called for a short jump. Adults jump four to five feet easily, and even mothers carrying infants have no difficulty leaping the chasm. But when the mother with her child walking alongside reached the space between the branches, she bent down and the youngster climbed on her back before she jumped to the next tree. One juvenile reached the end of the limb and hesitated to make the jump from one swaying branch to the other. An adult female, holding the branch with her tail, swung out into space and caught the wind-tossed limb of the next tree. The young creature, using the adult's body like a bridge, moved safely across the space and hurried to catch up with the group which by now had reached a tall fig tree and was enjoying its breakfast.

Steadied by their tails and feet, the howlers reach out and pull the leaves and fruit to their mouths where they eat directly from the branches. They would find it hard to break off the fruit with their hands, nor are they able to carry any fruit away to be eaten later. For about two hours the monkeys move about the feeding trees. Then, one by one, the adults find a safe comfortable resting place and, after curling their tails around a

24

branch to assure safety, they spend the next hours sleeping or grooming or just resting.

Babies nurse and are groomed and then climb over their mothers playing with leaves and twigs. The juveniles, full of pep, spend the middle of the day playing. A young howler swings from a limb by his tail. He is joined by others. Soon a scuffle starts, with feet and hands free for wrestling. When they are tired of their games they play follow-the-leader, and soon all eight youngsters are chasing along a definite circuit of branches, making small jumps, swinging by their tails and climbing up swaying vines. The young always play actively when not eating or sleeping or traveling with the troop. In this way they grow strong in play-fighting and climbing practice. After the first three years, life becomes more serious and their play time ends.

25

There is a cry of distress and all the adults leave their resting positions and rush to the aid of a young howler who, on his first adventure away from his mother's side, had slipped from a limb and was clinging to a thin branch sixty feet below. Piercing cries come from the frightened monkey. Several adults swing down headfirst on the long vines to within twenty feet of the fallen youngster, barking encouragement all the time. The mother holds a vine tightly with her toes and descends as near as she can to the baby. It isn't near enough. She rocks back and forth, putting the vine into motion and then, swinging nearer, she catches the top of the swaying sapling and reaches out for her frightened infant who then climbs to her back. Together they rejoin the watching clan.

After all this activity the animals begin to feel hungry again and move toward another feeding tree for an afternoon meal. The supply on the tree nearby is not exhausted, but they seem to want a change of diet. They stop about a hundred yards away to eat fresh buds and leaves. A female dips her finger in a pool of water collected in a hollow between branches. She licks the water from her fingers and hurries to catch up with her companions.

There is a sound of breaking branches in the next tree and a single strange male howler appears. A vocal battle takes place. All the males howl and roar and the females bark and whine. The noise is accompanied by much shaking of the branches and can be heard for miles. There is no fighting and after a while the intruder disappears in the dense foliage.

When disturbed, howler monkeys react in various ways. Usually the males rush forward with loud roars and then break off branches which they drop on the intruder if he is below them. The females remain quiet and often hide in the thick leaves. In places where howlers have been hunted by man, the entire clan

26

becomes silent and disappears into the tops of the trees, well out of sight.

The clan shares its feeding tree with a group of capuchin monkeys who had already arrived, but pay no attention to them. When the capuchins are finished, they move swiftly away, traveling fifteen hundred yards without stopping. They have little in common with the slow-progressing howlers, each kind going its separate way. Howler monkeys bother even less with the quick, red spider monkeys who share their territory, while they rarely ever encounter the marmosets, since these small monkeys prefer the scrub forest below and their paths do not often cross.

The afternoon feeding lasts until six—when a grunt from a male leader brings the clan together and the group moves on in the usual single-file formation toward a lodge tree a hundred yards away. They progress leisurely, running along the tree limbs, swinging across an opening on a vine. At one chasm a male holds two swaying branches together so that a hesitant, young monkey can pass over to another tree. During the whole day long they have not traveled more than five hundred yards.

Before nightfall the monkeys all become very excited when they discover a female with a newborn baby in her arms, holding onto a branch with her tail and hind feet and licking clean the light brown baby. It struggles in her arms, but the mother holds the squirming infant by its tail as she carefully looks it over. A circle of females and juveniles stand around watching, trying to touch the new addition to their clan. Finally she presses the baby to her breast and with a soft purring sound the infant has his first meal.

By nightfall, the howler monkeys are sprawled in a lodge tree, with their tails tightly coiled around branches for safety. Many have their heads resting on their arms and their feet dangling, while others straddle the branches with both arms and legs dangling. Mothers hold their babies nestled close in their long hair. The young of other years cuddle close to their mothers' backs, attempting to keep warm and find protection from the wind. The monkeys settle quietly to sleep until dawn, when they will again greet the day with the loud howling that has given them their name.

CAPUCHIN

You have probably never seen an organ grinder with a little dressed-up monkey on a chain collecting pennies from onlookers

Capuchin monkey

The organ grinder's monkey

on the street corner. It is a vivid memory for many grownups, but the organ grinders and their monkeys are now gone forever.

The clever little brown and black fellow, who looked so aware and intelligent, was a capuchin monkey. You are familiar with his relatives because capuchins are the commonest monkeys in the zoo. But his real home is in Central and South America as far south as the Amazon rain forests, where small bands of capuchin monkeys wander about in the tall trees eating fruit and leaves, as well as birds' eggs, snails and insects. Capuchins, so named because of the cowl-like tufts of hair on their heads, have superior use of their hands and large, highly developed brains and intelligence comparable to that of the Old World monkeys.

Young capuchin

Capuchins can hang by their fully furred tails and use them to keep steady when on a limb, but cannot use them as grasping extra hands like the howlers. Because they carry their long tail curled downward in a spiral they are sometimes called "ringtails." The creatures are difficult to observe because they go so swiftly through the foliage, often traveling more than three-quarters of a mile without stopping, and making long jumps with ease. They pay no attention to the noisy howler monkeys which share their large territory, and they frequently stop to eat a few figs from a tree already occupied by spider monkeys, but always move on swiftly to other trees in the great canopy of the rain forest.

SPIDER MONKEYS

At daybreak the spider monkeys, awakened by the howler monkeys, add their terrier-like barks to the dawn serenade. But these little monkeys are hungry and they begin to travel immediately. They scatter over a large area and there is a continuous chatter that keeps the group together where it is impossible to see one another through the thick foliage. They streak along, swinging from branch to branch so rapidly that it is sometimes difficult to follow them. All the trees overhead appear to be filled with the movement of the group. They take death-defying leaps forward and downward of thirty feet or more, and catch hold of branches with their long hooklike fingers. They do not have opposable thumbs.

The monkeys scatter over the fruit trees, paying no attention to the howlers eating in the same trees, and chatter and eat until midmorning, when they rest in small groups until afternoon. The resting groups may be made up of a single female and her baby or of several females and their young; the old

and young males rest to-
gether without dividing into
age groups, which is unusual
in the monkey world.

All spider monkeys are
slim and have long arms and
legs (from which they get
their name). All have a long,
prehensile tail, a small head
with naked face, hardly any
thumbs, and straggly hair
which varies in color from
jet black to red.

The size of a troop varies
from about ten to forty individuals. Usually there are
about twice as many females
as males, all taking an active
part in group activities. In
one group of thirty-three individuals, resting after a
heavy meal, eight were adult
males, fifteen were adult females, four having infants
which they nurse and carefully groom; only the six juveniles seemed to need no
rest. The youngsters run and
jump from branch to branch,
and swing by arms or legs,
although usually with their
tails, thus leaving their limbs

Spider monkey

33

free for the inevitable wrestling matches.

Another troop of red spider monkeys approaches, but halts in a nearby tree. All the males and females of the first troop, ready to defend their territory, rush to the ends of the branches and face the intruders, barking loudly and shaking the breaking branches with their hands and feet. Then, for some unknown reason, the monkeys begin to scratch themselves vigorously, and soon the intruders pass by without making any trouble. It is small wonder that spider monkey territories overlap at the margins, for there may be as many as two hundred of these little monkeys within a square mile all through the rain forests from southern Mexico to Uruguay.

By afternoon the monkeys are hungry again and, with a female leading, start toward a cluster of nut trees. A mother presses a young baby to her belly where it clings tightly; another infant rides piggyback with its tail coiled around that of the mother and its feet pressed into her flanks, its hands grasping the hair on her sides. Young are rarely seen traveling alone on the difficult arboreal pathways. At one place a male stops long enough to hold together two branches so that a juvenile can cross over more easily. At another chasm an adult goes feet first down a swinging vine and then reaches out to hold the vine firmly against a tree trunk until five young animals descend and move safely to the tree. This was a difficult passage and one they could not have made by themselves. Somewhere along the line the young gain confidence and finally they, too, can make long jumps. With their feet and hands spread out, they will be able to drop and land safely onto a limb twenty-five feet below. Until that time there is always an adult to lend a hand.

The continual chattering keeps the scattered group together. When some of them get too far away and feel lost, they make a

Spider monkey against an early morning sun

whimpering sound like that of a horse, only very high pitched. An answering call soon reunites the troop. At nightfall they all settle down in their sleeping trees, often returning eight or ten nights to sleep in the same trees.

MARMOSET

Marmosets are so primitive that some scientists call them half-monkeys. They do not have prehensile tails and they have claws instead of nails on all their digits except the big toes. These small bright-eyed creatures live in the lower branches of the tall trees in the rain forests of the New World. They are high-strung, alert and curious, and they chatter like a flock of birds as they leap from branch to branch, feeding on insects, fruits and seeds. Some are as large as rats and another kind, called the pigmy marmosets, are as small as mice. Several pairs join together as a small group of eight or more, and when night comes they sleep close together, curled up with their tails over their heads.

When a marmoset becomes angry its fur stands on end, it makes faces and jerks its head from side to side, and it screams. But they do not mind the other kinds of monkeys that live above them in the trees, for they seem to know that they are friends.

Twins are usually born to these very small monkeys. Pigmy babies are about the size of navy beans when they are born, although their eyes are open and they are fully furred. The father marmoset carries the babies, one tucked in each groin where they are safe and warm. At nursing time he hands them over to the mother.

Golden marmoset

Red Uakaris

RED UAKARI

Red-faced Uakari monkeys travel in troops through the top-most branches of the rain forests bordering the Amazon River. No other monkey looks so queer. Its thin body is covered with long, straggly red hair. Its red face becomes even redder when the animal is excited. One kind of Uakari has a completely bald head; another has but a few bristles on the forehead; while another has a whorl of hair on the top of the head. They are about two feet tall and all have a most woebegone expression. They have only a stump of a tail, but extremely long, slender, pink fingers and toes. In the dense trees they find fruit, nuts and other seeds, as well as frogs and snails. Sometimes they even come down to the forest floor to collect fallen fruit.

5

Old World Monkeys

MACAQUES

RHESUS MONKEY

Do you know who took the first flight into space? A Rhesus monkey! The little monkey was shot up in a rocket and brought safely down again some time before a man was allowed to take the chance. But preceding man into space is not this animal's first service to mankind. Rhesus monkeys may have saved your life. Countless thousands of the small creatures were used in the research that produced the Salk vaccine for polio. Next time you stand in front of their cage at the zoo watching these sandy-colored monkeys with thin, naked flesh-colored faces and hands doing their acrobatics, remember to say a little thank-you for what their kind has done and continues to do for mankind. In India, their native land, the Hindu people hold these monkeys as sacred.

Rhesus monkeys travel about on the ground in bands of from 20 to 160. They have a highly developed social order in which each monkey has its own special place of rank, from the male leader, who holds his tail high and demands the respect of all the band, down to the young males at the bottom of the social scale who have the respect of none.

If you have any doubt about which Rhesus monkey in a group ranks first, you need only place some food in a clearing, and

Rhesus monkeys

watch what happens. The dominant male leader has indisputed right to first choice of the food, while the others look on. A few males lower in rank approach after a while and are allowed to eat. Next come the dominant females with their young, who outrank all the other females and even many adult males. All around the edge of the clearing the young males wait a chance to rush in, grab a piece of food and retire to a distance to eat. Daughters stay with their mothers for six years, but males three to five years old leave the center of the group to join the other young males at the lowest place in the social order.

The rules of the social order are so well defined that each monkey gives up its sitting place at once when a member higher up in the order approaches, and all get up to offer a seat to the dominant male. Disputes are apt to arise from time to time, but they are usually settled through signals. The system works like this: One monkey may threaten another just by staring at it, or by simply raising its eyebrows or lowering its forehead, by bobbing its head up and down, or by repeated huffing, or it may actually rush forward with a snarl, pretending to attack. The monkey being threatened may just look the other way, or walk away, or just sit grinning in response to all the threats, to show that it is not afraid. You can see how hard it would be to start a fight if your opponent just sat and grinned, can't you? Usually the monkeys solve their differences without fighting, but if a squabble does get started, there is much excitement and all the band join in the fight.

41

Living by rigid social rules helps avoid much trouble. The troop seems to be held together by affection as well as their social rules—the love the mothers have for their infants, the juveniles have for each other in their play groups, and the affection the adult males seem to have for the young animals in the band.

When a troop stops to rest, the various members immediately begin to groom each other. The mothers hold their babies firmly and gently and clean their fur; the older males groom the immature youngsters; and while a few females groom the leader, the juveniles clean the fur of the females. It is like a beauty parlor where each person does the hair of another while being made beautiful herself.

This grooming is very important, for it holds the monkeys together in close physical contact and at the same time insures healthy, clean fur and skin for every member of the troop. The animals seem to get real pleasure from the activity as well.

When the grooming is finished, the youngsters get together to play, while the resting mothers watch and keep order. For the first couple of months the infant is not punished, but by the time it is five months old it has learned to try to avoid doing anything that calls for a cuff or a good shaking.

The youngsters climb trees and swing on hanging vines. They may dive as much as thirty feet from tree limbs into a small pond below, where they swim and splash each other, and then climb up to dive again and again.

When suddenly the leader, tail held high, climbs a nearby tree, the entire band becomes alert. A mother presses her clinging baby closer to her body, another female grins and her month-old infant runs to cling to her waist, ready for travel. The older youngsters leave the pond and climb to the backs of their mothers and, riding piggyback, disappear in the heavy foliage above.

While feeding, the band spreads out over about a fifty-yard area, but when dusk comes, the individuals draw close together and sleep in the tall treetops, often returning to the same trees for several nights in succession.

Rhesus monkeys are now being raised in the New World for scientific study on Cayo Santiago Island in the Caribbean. Altogether we owe much to these small monkeys for their service to mankind—in the past, present and future.

JAPANESE MONKEY

The calls of the Japanese monkeys can easily be heard as a troop travels swiftly through the dense forest on the mountainside collecting leaves, fruit and nuts. These monkeys live in the most northerly range of any monkeys and are so shy that one can rarely catch a glimpse of them, although they can be heard without difficulty as they forage over their home territory of two or three square miles, in troops of 30 to 200 individuals.

You can readily understand that you can't really study animals unless you can see them. Japanese scientists, finding a troop of these monkeys living on an island, decided to lure the creatures to an open space where they could be constantly observed at close distance. They built an observation shack on the beach and placed sweet potatoes and wheat grains on the rocks near the blind. It was not long before the greed for food overcame the animal's natural fear of man and the monkeys began to feed in full view of the scientists.

Names were given to each monkey and individual records were kept in each case. At such close range the scientists were able to study the vocal sounds that accompanied the actions of the monkeys. They were able to distinguish thirty different sounds, and discovered that some troops were noisier than oth-

Japanese monkeys

ers and that large troops usually had a larger vocabulary than smaller troops. The most interesting discovery was that certain sounds had the same meaning in every group. Finally, the researchers were able to produce sounds which were answered by the troop in the distance just as if the calls had been made by fellow monkeys.

Some sounds were low mutterings heard only nearby; others were high pitched and loud and carried far through the dense forest. When *kwaa* is called by one monkey, the answering call is *jii*, and at once the whole troop begins to move away. Other sounds are highly emotional: *ga-ga-ga* is a threat and is followed by tree shaking or actual attack. When the strongest monkey in the troop utters the warning call of *kuan*, all the others disappear silently among the leaves overhead. The leader remains in the top of a tree to observe the intruder until the troop is safely away.

45

Much was also learned about Japanese monkey society. The center of each troop is made up of one or several leading males and all the females and their babies. Sub-leader males and juveniles form the edge around the center group.

To find the real leader of a troop, the scientists threw a sweet potato between two males. The leader takes the food while the other monkey, lower on the social scale, looks the other way, pretending he hasn't seen the food at all. When a monkey is seen to move away, giving his place to another monkey, it is because the newcomer is higher in their society. In the Japanese monkey troop the leaders and sub-leaders never quarrel among themselves but together protect the females and young and guard them when they are traveling through the treetops, also making sure that they get food.

During the mating season the faces and other parts of both sexes become a bright scarlet. Babies walk about when they are a week or so old, but stay with their mothers for about ten months. When a new baby arrives, the male leader or one of the sub-leaders takes over the care of the older youngster so the mother can give all her attention to the newborn. The child of a dominant female is higher in the social order than the other females and the leader male always takes over the care of the child in this case. He grooms it, hugs it, walks it, and gives it special protection. This care given by the male Japanese monkey to the young is rarely found in other monkey societies.

After they are eight months old, all youngsters in the troop play together. In the second year, the juvenile males spend more and more time visiting with the young males on the fringe of the social group, until finally they leave the protected center and become a part of this lowest group in the social scale. Many become leaders and later return to the center, when they are much older. The female young never leave the center. They mature when three-and-a-half years old and raise their own young in the well-protected center of the troop.

You can see that after a dozen years of observation, the scientists came to know each monkey individually and also the kinship of each monkey to another in one troop of sixty-one monkeys living on the forest-covered island of Kushima. They discovered some startling things about how the Japanese monkeys learned new habits and how these were then passed on to others in the group. It may be that this is the same way in which early man first learned and shared knowledge in the beginning of our own human society.

One day Emo, an eighteen-month-old female monkey, found a sweet potato along the bank of a stream of fresh water that ran into the sea. The potato was covered with sand and by chance she put it into the nearby stream and washed off the sand with her hands. She must have liked the result for she continued to clean her sweet potatoes before eating them. A month

Emo dips her potato in the sea and seems to like the salty taste

47

later, a playmate followed her example and washed his food when he saw Emo washing hers. Four months later, Emo's mother began washing her potatoes, too. This practice of potato washing eventually spread through the troop until, after ten years, this washing, started by the young Emo, was a regular part of their normal feeding behavior. Only the old males did not acquire the habit.

When the scientists first began their study, all the monkeys ran on all fours when they came to the ground to get the food, and did not enter the water at all. Later, in order to carry potatoes in their hands, they began to run toward the water on their hind legs. At first all the washing was done in the fresh water stream, but later the monkeys began to wash their potatoes in the sea. Perhaps they enjoyed its salty seasoning, for soon they began to nibble the clean potato, then dip it again in the salty water before taking another bite.

When Emo was four years old she invented another practice that spread to the other animals in the troop. The scientists scattered wheat on the ground to supplement the other food of the monkeys. At first, the monkeys picked it up grain by grain and ate sand as well. One day the clever Emo was seen to scoop up a handful of wheat and sand and throw it onto the water, where the wheat separated from the sand, so that she could easily eat the clean wheat. Her playmates followed her example and the habit soon spread throughout the troop.

Now another not-so-nice practice began to show up for the first time. Some cunning monkeys attacked the clever monkeys that were washing wheat and took advantage of another's labor to get their food. One mother and daughter never learned to wash wheat, but always stole from the others.

From not going near the water at first the monkeys were now wetting their hands and feet in the sea—which would have been

Finally, most of the troop learned to wash food

a big step in itself. The scientists wanted to see if these monkeys would finally lose their fear of the water altogether, so they threw peanuts into the deep water. The younger monkeys at once jumped into the water to get the peanuts, and before long they walked into the sea in the heat of the day just to cool off. It was not long after that they were swimming and diving for seaweed out of pure pleasure, although the older individuals in the troop did not learn to swim. All of the animals had to walk upright in order to carry their food to the sea for washing, and so more and more the creatures ran about on two feet even when their hands were free.

This close scientific study has shown how the Japanese monkeys learn and pass on their habits to others in the troop. New infants imitated the new culture habits so quickly it almost seemed that they were born with the knowledge of washing potatoes and wheat. The sea, no longer feared, became a playground for all.

49

LANGURS

Langurs live in the forests of India and the Orient. They come in a variety of sizes and colors and shapes, but all langurs are extremely lanky and have very long tails. One kind of langur travels through the tops of the very tallest trees and rarely if ever comes down to the ground. Little is known of their private lives. Another kind—large, brownish, and with a jet-black face, ears, hands and feet—lives on the sides of mountains in the upper limits of the tree range and sometimes is even observed playing about on the snow. The lovely, capped langur is small and has hair that grows smoothly backward, falling about the neck like a cape.

The Indian langurs spend much time on the ground and in the lower branches of trees, so that we know more about how they live. Indeed, one scientist became so friendly with these monkeys that he was able to follow a certain troop all day long, resting when they did, until he was finally accepted to such a degree that the animals climbed over him trying to groom him as though he were one of their own.

At sunrise the langurs wake and become active. They move about eating leaves. Leaf food is always so abundant that there is little need to show who is boss or leader, and so the adult males are usually as relaxed as the other members of the troop. There is also little need for fighting. Yet the adult males highest up in the social order do lead in defending the troop and in keeping peace, as well as warding off strange male monkeys who try to join the troop.

When all are satisfied and every baby has been nursed, an adult starts off through the trees and the other troop members, numbering anywhere from fifteen to fifty, follow along with the females and young in the center, protected by front and rear

Langur monkeys

guards. The adult monkey traveling first along the pathway is the leader for the time being and may be either male or female. They follow no regular trails. When the foliage is dense, the langurs stay close together, but they spread out to forage when the forest is more open.

Tired from the early morning foraging, the troop of monkeys stops to rest on the ground, in the shade. This is the time for relaxing and grooming and for play. The females crowd around a mother with a new baby, begging to be allowed to hold the newest member of the troop. Each new baby causes great excitement among the females, who want to caress and fondle it, although the males pay no attention whatever to the infant. Several mothers sit quietly nursing their young, gently stroking and grooming the soft, dark fur.

51

Capped langur with young

There is a close contact of mother and infant for the first month. After two weeks, the baby knows the difference between his mother and other doting females, and will cry out to her if she comes near. The baby will even take a few faltering steps to meet her. All its waking hours are spent clinging to her or nursing or climbing over her while she rests. If the baby strays away, its mother reaches out to catch it by its leg or tail.

A month-old baby, having finished nursing, begins to explore. It smells and touches and tastes every twig and leaf nearby. It trips over its tail and lets out a squeak. Then the mother is quick to reach out to give support and comfort. A two-and-a-half-month-old youngster wanders only about ten feet away, and whenever the mother taps on the ground the baby runs quickly to her side.

A female stays in charge of a group of light gray, three-to-five-month-olds who climb all over her in their play. When one gets too far away she reaches out to pull it back to the group.

Older youngsters run and jump and climb, and wrestle and pull each other's tails.

53

They are three- and four year-olds that have already learned not to squeal or else a male will come and break up the rough play. One youngster spies the hanging tail of an adult who rests on a limb of a tree and starts to swing on it. A new game has started and all join in the fun. At first, the adult doesn't seem to mind, but when he has had enough, one grunt puts a stop to the game.

These are relaxed and happy, easy-going monkeys. Suddenly in the distance, however, there is a strange roar. An adult male barks sharply. The young scamper to their mothers. The new mother presses her baby to her belly, where it clings tightly. She and the other squealing females then disappear in the treetops, followed by the rest of the males who form the rear guard. In a matter of seconds the langurs are all far away.

When angry, these usually peaceful monkeys stare and grind their teeth and slap the ground. When the males get really excited they crash through the branches, jump to the ground with great whooping sounds, and then leap up into the trees to crash about again. But when all is calm they greet each other with affection, throwing their arms about each other and putting their heads on the others' chests.

During the day the langur troops moves about a mile within their three-to-five-mile home range. They sleep wherever darkness finds them, sitting upright in trees with their legs propped against the limb for support. Their heads rest on their knees and their arms are wrapped around their legs. All of the troop sleep close together, with the young warm and safe in the mothers' laps.

BABOONS

Baboons, the bulkiest of all monkeys, are generally peaceful, friendly and affectionate. They graze on the African plains, alongside the gazelles who have highly developed senses of hearing and smell and are consequently extremely alert to danger. The baboons, with their especially good eyesight, are constantly on the watch while they are eating. This association makes an excellent arrangement, for a warning bark of a baboon alerts all the animals nearby and a quick toss of a gazelle's head sends the baboons to the nearest treetops for safety.

Baboons live in troops of from ten to over a hundred, but usually there are about forty who stay together all their lives. They travel, eat and sleep together. No individual wanders more than a few feet away from another baboon any time in its life, for safety lies in the protection of the troop.

The largest adult in a troop weighs about seventy pounds and is the dominant male or leader. He has long teeth and pow-

Baboons eating

erful jaws and a long, heavy mantle of hair. All decisions are made by this leader and if he has any trouble keeping order he calls on several other strong fighting males who back him up at all times.

Females, half the size of the males, have shorter teeth and thinner mantles. They come after the leader and the strong males in the social order, along with the young animals. It is into this well-organized pattern that the small, black, infant baboon is born. For the first few months it clings tightly to the hair of its mother's chest, even when she is traveling with the troop. During these early weeks the mother spends much of her time grooming her infant, while the other females crowd about her, making over the new baby. When a few months old, the infant climbs to its mother's back and holds on to her long back hair. By the time it is nine months it has already grown a brown coat of hair of its own and it now sits upright on her back and rides along jockey fashion.

The troop moves about over its territory of two to four square

56

Baboon sleeping

miles, although often a larger area, eating plants, buds and fruit. Blades of grass are pulled up and each is then rubbed clean before it is eaten. The grassland is a good territory, for it fills all the needs of the troop—plenty of food and water holes conveniently placed for visiting every day during the dry season. There are clumps of trees scattered about in which to find safety for the night, as well as to run to when a warning bark is given by the leader.

The troop always moves in a certain order, with the front guard made up of adult males and the larger juveniles, followed by the females and their young. The mother with the new baby travels in the center, with the large strong leader close by as a special guard. The rear guard is composed of the rest of the males and juveniles. In this way the mother and baby are well protected. When she finds it hard to keep up with the troop and drops behind, the leader slows up and walks by her side to protect her and the baby until she can catch up again.

The troop pays no attention to the antelopes and giraffes grazing nearby. They are also aware that hyenas and jackals

are afraid of them and usually keep their distance. But at the approach of another troop of baboons, the females and young hurry along to the safety of the treetops. The males slowly close in their ranks and there is a great noise of barking and ground slapping. Usually the intruders know when they are outnumbered and turn away, but if not, then a fight begins and the animals charge one another, baring their great tearing teeth. But let a lion come near and one shrill bark from the leader sends the whole baboon troop into flight. Then, from the safety of the top branches of the nearest trees, they only roar and threaten, for they know when they have met their match.

When on the move, a troop of baboons stops often to rest and groom—an activity at which they spend several hours each day throughout their lives. Hair is carefully parted with the hands and all dirt and bugs are removed, with much smacking of lips. Mothers groom their infants, adult females groom the males and one another. Besides being pleasurable, relaxing and cleansing, the grooming keeps the animals in close contact with each other.

Of course, the leader gets most of the attention, both in

grooming and when feeding. Whenever he approaches, a subordinate baboon grins at him and moves out of the way. There is no real fighting for position. If the leader is threatened, a single bark brings all the males to back him up. Indeed, if any bickering starts in the baboon troop the leader runs to stop it. In this way the weaker animal is always protected within the troop.

When not eating or being groomed, the young baboons come together in a play group. They climb, jump, tumble, pull tails and chase each other. In this way they develop physical strength and also learn to get along with other baboons. They play silently with rarely a sound, but when the activity gets too rough and an animal screeches, the dominant male comes running to stop the rough play. It is a happy time, for they play hard and then relax completely.

Long before it is dark the baboon troop seeks the safety of the treetops. They know that with darkness their greatest enemies come out to hunt for food. There is much grunting as the troop is called close together. They sleep in the trees in a sitting-up position. They may use the same trees for several nights or they may find another group of trees near where they happen to be when night falls.

When full daylight comes again, the leader gives the signal and the troop begins to move about again. Another day has arrived and the creatures are hungry.

MANDRILL

Mandrills, like other baboons, live on the ground, but they prefer the wet forests of Africa and only occasionally make forages out into open country and among the rocks at the foot

59

Mandrills

of the mountain, searching for snakes and insects to add to their
fruit and root diet. Adult males have brilliant, blue-ribbed
cheeks and bright red noses and buttocks. Females are smaller
and less brightly colored, and young males have black-ribbed
faces.

60

The Hamadryads were the sacred baboons of ancient Egypt, Abyssinia and Arabia. The animals were trained to pick fruit and when they died, their bodies were mummified (especially treated) like Egyptian kings. The creatures are grayish in color, large and powerfully built, and possess manes that cover their forebodies. They live in troops traveling on the ground. They dig for roots and even turn over stones in search of insects, lizards and snails. These baboons have the speed of horses and can defend themselves against their enemies, the leopards. A troop of hamadryads have been known to make surprise raids on other baboon troops, taking prisoners in a manner almost like organized warfare.

Hamadryad

ALLEN'S SWAMP MONKEY

These small, grayish-green monkeys have light gray ruffs around their necks and almost black faces and hands. They travel in troops in the swamp areas of the dense, dark Congo forests. Living near water, it is not a wonder these monkeys are good swimmers and that they spend much time catching small fish and shrimp to add to their diet of fruit and nuts.

A young one climbs over its mother, biting her in fun, but when she has had enough, she gives the baby a cuff. Sometimes in play young swamp monkeys hang from the branches by their hind legs.

Allen's swamp monkey

Proboscis monkeys

PROBOSCIS MONKEY

This monkey is named for its huge flesh-colored nose which grows from a snub nose at birth to a long spoon-shaped one of three inches at maturity. Some old males even have noses that extend below their chins. The set of their mouths make them appear to be grinning. Proboscis monkeys have quite unusual coloring in the monkey world, for their heads are bright red and their bodies are rusty red shading to buff below. The dense mangrove forests of Borneo give them good protection and the mangrove leaves, shoots and fruit offer abundant food.

Like all tree monkeys, they travel in troops and their progress

63

can be seen and heard. They shake the limbs as they move along in the tree tops and make long drops from high to lower branches, crashing through the foliage, often falling. Their cries of *honk* and *kee-honk* sound like notes played on the bass viol. In the early morning and late afternoon the animals climb to the tops of the trees, probably to soak in the heat of the sun, for they cannot stand any cold at all. Yet in the hottest part of the day you will find them resting in the shade on the ground.

LION MONKEY

These unusually shy forest animals wear glossy black coats and have long gray hair framing their faces, making them look like lions.

Lion monkey

DeBrazza Guenon monkey

DEBRAZZA GUENON

This small monkey lives in the Congo rain forest eating fruit, leaves and insects. It possesses cheek pouches, which is most unusual for a monkey. This baby, left alone for a moment, seeks the comfort of thumbsucking.

PATAS MONKEY

Large groups of reddish-brown patas monkeys run about on the scrublands of West Africa on their doglike legs.

COLOBUS MONKEY

Colobus monkeys live in Africa and travel in bands in the treetops, eating leaves, but always staying near the water. Although the amount of white varies, these large animals are usually jet black and white, with white bands across the brows, white cheeks and chin, and white tips at the ends of their four-foot tails. They are hunted for the long, black and white fur of their capes.

6

The Great Apes

The great apes, the highest of all the primates, next to man, were once widely spread through the warmer parts of the Old World. Now, only four kinds survive—the chimpanzees and gorillas in the forests of Africa and the orangutans and gibbons in the forests of Southeast Asia and nearby islands.

They are all fairly large creatures, without tails and with large brains. They have hands with an opposable thumb, for grasping, although not one so well made as your own. Even their feet have an opposable big toe and can be used for holding a banana or some other object. Compared with ourselves, the apes have relatively long arms and short legs; their eyes appear small and set closer together; their lips are long, thin and mobile. They lack true speech, although they do communicate with one another by means of calls and by various facial expressions.

Gorillas and chimpanzees spend most of their time on the ground, orangutans most of their time in the treetops, but the gibbon is remarkable as a tree-living acrobat that can race through the trees, swinging and jumping as it goes.

CHIMPANZEE

We are all familiar with the chimpanzee, for we often see these intelligent apes on stage or screen, dressed in clothes like our own and doing the things we like to do, such as skating and

Young chimpanzee

riding bicycles. We watch them eating with forks, drinking from glasses, using a napkin to wipe their lips, and we smile at the clever way they copy our actions.

We also see chimpanzees at the zoo and, because they have managed to survive and produce their young in cages, we are inclined to think we know how they live. Yet this is a mistake, for all we actually know from studying these attractive apes in confinement is how they have adjusted to a very strange way of life, as though we were studying men in prison.

Chimpanzees are really creatures of the wild, and only there can their true nature and behavior be appreciated. Scientists go to their home territories in Africa and study them in their natural surroundings. Once there, a suitable spot has to be found from which the chimpanzees can be observed. It is not enough to listen to their loud calls. They must be followed through the woods until dusk. Every movement must be watched, notes must be made, and photographs taken whenever possible. Moreover, the scientist must remain unobserved as he watches the apes eating, sleeping, resting and playing. He may have to watch for weeks or even for many months before he can recognize individual animals on sight.

One scientific team found a suitable place in the Congo where a troop of chimpanzees lived on a wooded hillside, except when they came out into the open to feed from a plantation of paw-paw trees. In most areas, chimpanzees have been pushed so far back into the dense forest that they are hard to find, but at this particular place the natives are superstitious and believe that if they throw a spear at a chimpanzee, the animal will catch it and hurl it back, killing the hunter. So the chimpanzees are left alone and the creatures wander freely from hillside to feeding ground. It was here in the Congo that the scientists constructed an observation blind on the ground and also high up in the treetops, where daily observations could be made of the chimpanzee activities in their natural forest home.

The single troop appeared to be divided into two distinct groups, an adult group consisting of twenty males and females but with no youngsters, and a second sub-group composed of about fifteen mothers and young, which the scientists called the nursing group.

Loud screams echoed through the forest on the hillside as the members of the adult group approached the edge of the clearing, but silence suddenly fell when they arrived there. One by one, the apes peered out from the protecting undergrowth before stepping out into the open. Walking upright, they turned in every direction; then, when all was seen to be safe, they put on a deafening display. They chased wildly up and down, shrieking and screaming, slapping the ground with their hands and stomping with their feet, like children suddenly let out to play. They slapped tree trunks and broke off branches which they waved wildly above their heads. (One scientist watched just such a display during a thunderstorm.) Then, abruptly, the animals became silent, climbed the pawpaw trees and busily set about eating the fruit. With their hunger satisfied, the chimpanzees finally returned to the wooded area and disappeared, carrying fruit in their arms.

Sometimes the adult group was not seen for days on end, perhaps because a ripe fig tree had been found in some other place, for the grown males especially range far afield in their search for food. The chimpanzees of the nursing group, on the other hand, arrived regularly at the pawpaw plantation, approaching the clearing silently and slowly along well-worn woodland paths. They were shy and extremely cautious, and careful not to expose their babies to any sort of risk. The mothers climbed the pawpaw trees with their young, often three or four years old, clinging to their back or belly. When the fruit had been picked, they carried it in their arms and walked upright to the edge of the clearing to eat it, where, at the slightest sound, they could immediately and silently disappear into the protection of the forest.

Chimpanzees behave differently in different parts of the African forests. Many spend a great deal of their time in the treetops; others climb into the trees only to get food or gain protection. Some kinds make their sleeping platforms on the ground, while others build them in the trees. Some chimpanzees are much noisier than others, and not only indulge in wild calling, but drumming and tree shaking as well. This is not a display of hostility but is associated with excitement, particularly when two groups meet, or when they answer the calls of distant chimpanzees, or when they announce loudly to all who can hear that they have found a tree loaded with ripe fruit. They call a noisy good-night, and an equally loud good-morning when they awake.

Perhaps this loud form of communication is a reason why groups of chimpanzees do not have a rigid social structure. There is no need for a dominant leader. When a chimpanzee utters an angry *wraaah*, it is a fearful sound that echoes through the forest, and the other chimpanzees take notice. In the troop

Chimpanzees

that was studied, it was an old gray-haired male that was treated with the greatest respect, not the most powerful member of the troop. He took no part in the displays, but appeared always to be watching over the group like a wise old man, and even the largest of the males gave him their respect.

In this same troop the mothers rested quietly, nursing and grooming their young. Even three-year-olds were being nursed. Older youngsters silently played tag and chased about, but always kept within sight of the nursing mothers. When a large bird flew overhead, a very young chimpanzee seeing it jumped up and down excitedly, without making a sound. Another child sat with hand outstretched, quietly begging for a bite of the fruit its mother was eating. One youngster finished nursing, climbed a sapling and began to bend the branches over to make a platform. By playing in this way he learns necessary skills before he becomes an adult. A three-year-old tries to break off a branch, but only manages to bend it. The mother reaches up and breaks off the limb, and the child then waves it above his head as he has often seen adults do in their display. In this silent nursery the mothers thus mold their young for the first eight or nine years. Young chimpanzees are happy and pampered. They never whine nor whimper, but always obey quickly.

When it is time to move on, a mother glances at a baby by her side, the infant climbs onto her back and off they go through the bushes. Another reaches out to tap her child on the shoulder to get its attention and this one also hastily climbs onto its mother before departure. The animals communicate by look and gesture, without use of voice, and there is perfect understanding. Silently, all the mothers, with their young riding jockey fashion, disappear into the underbrush. Their siesta is over. They move quietly along, although when the nursing group meets the adult group there is much noisy excitement and

This chimpanzee uses a tool to dig out insects

obvious pleasure. As they continue together and come to a fork in the path, the leading male stops, scratches his chest and seems to consider which way to proceed, but only for a moment, and then off they go.

A woman scientist in another part of Africa has made some new observations on the chimpanzee. Chimpanzees had been thought to be vegetarians that only occasionally ate a small lizard or a snail, but she saw one kill and start to eat a bushbuck larger than itself. She also saw a chimpanzee pick up a heavy stick and use it as a club. Perhaps chimpanzees use such clubs as weapons to defend themselves when attacked by a leopard.

Chimpanzees settled for the night

One chimpanzee used a large leaf as a napkin to wipe off sticky fingers, and another used crumpled leaves as a sponge to get drinking water that had collected in the crotch of a tree. But the scientist's most important discovery was that chimpanzees actually do use sticks and leaves, as tools and may even fashion such a tool for a special use. She saw one chimpanzee poke a thin stick into a termite nest to collect the tasty insects, which he then licked off the stick. Moreover, when a suitable stick could not be found, a chimpanzee stripped the leaves from a branch and made his own instrument for digging out termites. He could not have done this without having hands very much like your own.

But let's go back to the Congo troop we were watching. The day is drawing to a close and there are other things to do. As the chimpanzees moved on down the path to find their last meal of fruit for the day, a large male is seen to stand still for a long time, looking at the changing colors of the sunset sky, gazing so long that he has to run to catch up with his companions.

When twilight comes, the chimpanzees construct nests wherever they happen to be. They may build eighty feet above the ground, or sometimes down on the ground if they feel secure from the leopards that prowl at night. After choosing a suitable fork in a tree, each adult sets to work, bending thick, strong branches forward over the crotch and holding them in place with a foot. Then he tucks in the leafy twigs that stick out around and finally settles down on the platform to eat the snack he has carried up to bed. After a while he reaches out for more branches to push in here and there to make the bed more comfortable.

In their own nests the mothers nurse their young. Older children snuggle close to their mothers' sides for warmth. Darkness finds all the chimpanzees in the troop sleeping soundly.

74

ORANGUTAN

A family of orangutans travels along the swaying branches of the tall trees of the dense swampy forests that line the rivers of Borneo and Sumatra. The male, twice the size of the females, weighs 300 pounds and swings on powerful arms that have a span of over seven feet. His face is encircled by a wide, heavy cheek pad. Every now and then he blows up a sac in his throat and makes a loud burping sound. The two females and their young stay near him, continually calling so that even in the dense foliage they remain always in touch.

All the orangutan family have thick, red-orange hair that not only keeps them warm but sheds the water when it rains. In

Orangutan

75

Orangutan youth

spite of being heavy, they move rapidly and lightly through the
treetops, making use of their grasping feet for gripping and
climbing limbs in search of their favorite fruit, that of the durian
trees. Orangutans have been known to travel long distances to
obtain this fruit as it ripens. They pause long enough to nibble
tender leaves and to smack their lips over a real treat of birds'
eggs. Their faces are forever changing, continually producing
new expressions which may be a means of communicating with
one another when the family group is close together.

Suddenly there is a loud scream from one infant held close in
its mother's arms. This is the signal to stop and rest while the
mother nurses the hungry baby. A youngster, perhaps eighteen
months old, is not tired and continues to play along the swing-

ing branches nearby while the adults groom themselves. After the baby is satisfied the mother carefully cleans and combs its hair. She even bites off the little nails that have grown too long.

When all are rested, the "wild men of the woods," which is the meaning of the name, orangutan, swing off on their powerful arms. They have no fear of animals attacking them, for they have no enemies except man. Man, however, has killed or captured so many orangutans to send to zoos all over the world that there is a real danger of these creatures becoming extinct during your lifetime.

Orangutans rarely descend to the forest floor, for on the ground they are awkward and almost helpless on their short,

Baby orangutans

weak legs. Their feet, so good at gripping limbs, are nearly useless in walking because they do not flatten out like a proper foot.

When dusk falls, the male, and each female too, begins to make a rough sleeping platform by bending branches forward to a crotch of a tree and then sitting on them. Slowly the large animal turns about in a circle until all the leaves are packed down. Then he reaches out for more branches and tucks them under until the bed is soft and secure, and at last he settles down quietly, after a few grunts.

A soft rain falls. The tiny baby is held close and warm in its mother's arms. The older youngster cuddles close to its mother for warmth and dryness. Except for an occasional cry from the baby when it becomes uncomfortable or hungry, the orangutan family sleeps soundly throughout the rainy night.

GIBBON

The gibbon, the smallest and most agile of the apes, is also thought by many to be the cleanest, the gentlest and possibly the most intelligent. Native people often adopt a gibbon in the home and treat it as one of their own children. But by their very nature the gibbons' real home is in the tallest trees of Thailand and Malaya, where they swing gracefully hand over hand through the branches at a surprising speed. Their arm span is six feet and when in a hurry, the gibbon may leap thirty feet, catch a swinging branch and be out of sight in a second.

Gibbons are lightly built and are extremely agile acrobats. They move about the treetops in small family groups over a home range of about 160 acres. Males greet each day with loud hoots and calls which may last for three hours. All other gibbons are made aware of the group's exact location in the forest and warned to stay at a distance.

After the morning concert the family swings through the branches in trapeze fashion in search of fruit, particularly durian fruit, for breakfast, often using their feet to carry extra fruit with them as they travel along.

Males and females alike are very protective of their young and take turns carrying them and helping the half-grown youngsters across long gaps in the forest treeways. Males pay especial attention to the male juveniles, play with them and sit and groom them when they stop to rest. In fact, the gibbon family is close and affectionate. When being groomed, the gibbon grunts with satisfaction. Adults embrace one another in greeting, moving their tongues in and out and giving little twittering squeals. A male, when really excited, shows off with his acrobatics.

Gibbon ape

79

When a gibbon family chances to meet another group in their travels, there follows much head shaking and staring, accompanied by noise with both the male and female joining in with loud whoops. This battle of noise and bluff continues until one side gives up and backs away. The noise apparently takes the place of actual combat and is a much better way to solve difficulties than with tooth and nail.

Gibbons swing like trapeze artists on the end papers of this book.

GORILLA

The early morning sunlight reaches the tall trees on the mountainside and falls upon a group of gorillas sleeping soundly on their platform nests in the trees. A large male, the leader, sits

Gorilla

80

up and yawns. When he sees that the day promises to be a clear one he rises up on his short but powerful legs and stretches. Then he looks around at the dense African forest, his homeland. Hard rains have left the forest sodden and steaming. Although the central highland is perhaps the loveliest region of Africa, man does not come here often because of the heat and humidity. The mountain side is covered with a canopy of bamboo trees about thirty-five feet tall under which herbs and vines grow in a tangled mass always available for food. Buffalo and elephants leave well-beaten trails in the vegatation.

Because of his gray hair the leader is called a "silverback." He weighs about 400 pounds and stands six feet high. This largest individual of the group has a massive head. His forehead is low, with bulging ridges overhanging his eyes. He beats his broad chest twice with his large hands and then leaves his platform of branches where he has spent the night.

A female sits up and lies down again. Another female reaches out for a leaf and eats it. Infants crawl over their mothers' fur. Three adult males, still young enough to have black hair (and so are called "blackbacks") awaken and leave their nests and start to feed slowly. In a very short time all the gorillas in the troop are awake and cluster about the silverback leader on the ground. His actions guide the troop all day. When he moves, they all move; when he rests, then all the animals rest.

He starts off down the slope and all the gorillas follow single file. There are nineteen animals in the group. Besides the leader there are three blackbacks over six years old, six mature females, five juveniles from three to six years old and four infants under three. They scatter as they reach a feeding place where they eat herbs, shrubs, fruit and tender shoots, smacking their lips loudly with satisfaction. They are not curious about exploring as they move about the dense tangle of vines and vegetation.

Because of their weight, gorillas cannot live in the treetops and so spend most of their time on the ground. They are primarily four-footed creatures. After taking a few steps upright they continue on all fours. But this is understandable, for in the tangle of vegetation in the rain forest even scientists studying the gorillas often have to proceed on all fours.

Gorillas climb trees cautiously and slowly, in order to eat, to rest and sometimes just to sit and look about. They never jump or run freely about in trees as the other apes do. They walk along a limb on all fours and are often seen to test a branch to see if it is strong enough to carry their weight. They walk up a tree trunk having no branches by using their short legs and long arms, with the body arched. And when they descend they come down as you would, feet first, chest facing the trunk, and slide hand over hand, using their feet as brakes. When a gorilla is frightened he never climbs a tree, but flees on foot, for he can travel fifteen to twenty miles an hour and thus easily outrun a man and almost any other forest creature except a leopard.

Gorilla beating his chest

The feeding group moves along slowly, pausing often to rest and look about. One female carries a baby in her arm and progresses in a three-legged fashion. In walking, gorillas place the backs of their hands flat on the ground, but stand up when eating, leaving their hands free for gathering the food.

After a couple of hours of foraging the leader stops and stretches out on the ground where the sun reaches through a gap in the tree ferns. All the other gorillas gather near him. Each adult animal builds a simple platform-like nest by tucking branches under him, making a ridge so that while he rests there will be no danger of his slipping down the steep side of the mountain.

A female still holding her infant in her left arm reaches for a large lobelia stalk, breaks off leaf custers, and then bends in a branch with her right hand. She shifts the baby to the other side and repeats, pushing handfuls of shrubs beneath her. She builds the rest nest in twenty-five seconds. A juvenile nearby completes his nest in forty-five seconds.

Mothers nurse and groom their babies. The adults groom themselves, holding their hair back with one hand and using the other for cleaning. Only for parts the animal cannot reach does he get assistance. A juvenile backs up to the silverback for a little help. With gorillas, grooming is casual, and soon many adults are fast asleep.

Juveniles wander away from the adults and play together. They run and wrestle and climb lobelia stalks and slide down again. They even have a "snake dance," holding on to the hairs of the one in front as they go up and down the slope. One infant puts a sprig of leaves on his head and walks about holding its head steady. Another lies on its back and shreds leaves that fall on his face and chest. A seven-month-old infant runs along a fallen tree and stands up and beats his chest. After an animal is

Gorilla strutting

six years old, however, there is no more play for him in the gorilla troop.

Gorillas are quite silent, although they do make soft grumbling sounds of contentment and make grunts to keep together when they have spread out to feed. Sometimes there are harsh grunts of annoyance and even barks and screams. An infant screeches when it feels left behind or lost, and chuckles when it plays. Blackbacks seem to go through a voice change, during which their barks come out like croaking sounds. A warning bark causes the females to grab their babies and stand up and look about.

As the long, midday rest comes to an end excitement spreads through the group. The silverback makes a loud *hu-hu* sound, plucks a leaf and puts it between his lips. The other animals move out of his way. He grabs an overhead branch, snaps it off and flings it twenty feet away. Then he starts beating his chest with his cupped fingers—striking about eight times—and at the same time swings one leg in the air. He then runs sideways for several feet, slapping at the bushes close by, and thumps the ground loudly with his palms. All of this display is performed in thirty seconds!

All gorillas make this display; females do a shorter version, and youngsters play at it when they slap their chests and grab branches. Why? We can only guess. It does call attention to the animal and it does alert the group when the leader displays. It could be just a way to let off tension. Perhaps it is something like what happens when we slap each other on the back as tension rises at a football game.

A blackback struts stiff-legged with his arms bent outward at the elbow. His steps are short and abrupt. He doesn't appear to be excited and he does not call out. He is just showing off, making himself look big and powerful and enjoying doing it.

By now the male leader discovers he is hungry and moves off

Gorillas preparing beds for the night

quickly, with the others following. Young babies are clasped in their mother's arms, older youngsters travel under their own power, but hold tightly to the hair on their mother's rump. One mother starts off without her baby. At his scream, she stops and waits for him to reach her. He runs by her side for a few steps and then swings up onto her back. In single file the gorilla troop disappears in the undergrowth.

By six o'clock the leader is tired and, after selecting a tree, climbs it and begins to construct his platform for the night. It is only ten feet above the ground, although sometimes he climbs as high as sixty feet. The platform is not like the simple resting one, but is an elaborate affair with bent branches and vines intertwined. It may be circular or oblong, but because of his size he needs one that is at least five feet by five.

Several minutes after the leader starts to build his platform, all the gorillas following his lead have constructed their own platforms and are settling down with grunts of satisfaction. A baby cries once and there are a few noisy yawns. The gorilla troop sleeps soundly on their platforms, which are used only once. There are plenty of trees on their mountain side and they sleep wherever night happens to find them.

Index

JACQUELYN BERRILL

was born in Kentucky, graduated from the University of Toledo, and did postgraduate study at New York University. She was a group social worker with teen-age girls in the Jackson and Lansing, Michigan, Y.W.C.A. before her marriage to Dr. N. J. Berrill, professor of zoology at McGill University, Montreal.

The Berrills have three children, Peggy, Elsilyn and Michael, ranging from college age to married. Now there is a new generation of young children to enjoy their grandmother's books. Besides keeping house and writing and illustrating her books, Mrs. Berrill makes jewelry. This new hobby she finds completely fascinating.